Spot the Difference

Feet

Diyan Leake

Heinemann Library
Chicago, Illinois

Customer Service 888-454-2279
Visit our website at www.heinemannraintree.com

Designed by Joanna Hinton-Malivoire
Printed in China by South China Printing Company Limited

12 11 10 09 08
10 9 8 7 6 5 4 3 2 1

ISBN-10: 1-4329-0000-5 (hc)
ISBN-10: 1-4329-0005-6 (pb)

The Library of Congress has cataloged the first edition as follows:
Leake, Diyan.
  Feet / Diyan Leake. -- 1st ed.
     p. cm. -- (Spot the difference)
  Includes bibliographical references and index.
  ISBN 978-1-4329-0000-7 (hc) -- ISBN 978-1-4329-0005-2 (pb)
  1. Foot--Juvenile literature. I. Title.
  QL950.7.L43 2007
  591.47'9--dc22
                              2007010530

Acknowledgments
The author and publisher are grateful to the following for permission to reproduce photographs: Alamy/Juniors Bildarchiv p. **8**; Animal Photography pp. **9**, **23** top; Digital Vision p. **18**, **back cover**; FLPA/Frans Lanting/Minden Pictures pp. **14**, **22**; FLPA/Martin B. Withers p. **11**; Jupiter Images/Workbook stock/Natural Moments Photography Ltd. p. **20**; Nature Picture Llibrary pp. **4** (Tony Heald), **5** (Staffan Widstrand), **6** (Simon King), **7** (Carol Walker), **10** (Tony Heald), **12** (Elliott Bignell), **16** (Pete Oxford), **22** (Pete Oxford); NHPA/Kevin Schafer pp. **15**, **23** middle; Photolibrary/Animals Animals/Earth Scenes p. **17**; Photolibrary/Imagestate Ltd. p. **21**; Photolibrary/Michael Fogden pp. **13**, **23** bottom; Photolibrary/Satyendra K. Tiwari p. **19**.

Cover photograph of the feet of a blue-footed booby reproduced with permission of Getty Image/National Geographic (Timothy Laman).

Every effort has been made to contact copyright holders of any material reproduced in this book. Any omissions will be rectified in subsequent printings if notice is given to the publisher.

Contents

What Are Feet?

Many animals have feet.

Many animals have feet on the end
of legs.

Why Do Animals Have Feet?

Animals use their feet to stand.

Animals use their feet to run.

Different Feet

Feet come in many shapes.
Feet come in many sizes.

8

This is a dog.
It has furry feet.

This is an elephant.
It has big feet.

This is a bird.
It has small feet.

This is a snail.

It has one foot.

This is a frog.
It has webbed feet.

Amazing Feet

This is a gecko.

It has feet that stick.

This is a sloth.

It has feet like hooks.

blue-footed booby

This is a bird.
It has blue feet.

This is a lizard.
It has fast feet.

This is an ape.

It can climb with its feet.

This is a butterfly.
It can taste with its feet.

Your Feet

People have feet, too.

People use their feet to move.
People are like other animals.

Spot the Difference!

Which animal has feet that stick?

Which animal has webbed feet?

Picture Glossary

 **furry** has lots of soft hair

 **hook** something bent that can be used to hang onto things

 **webbed** has skin that joins its toes together

Index

Note to Parents and Teachers

Before reading

Talk to the children about their feet. Help them find their toes, heel, sole, ankle, big toe, and toenails. Ask them to think about animals' feet. Do all animals have toes? Do all animals have nails?

After reading

- Place some plastic sheeting on the floor and then place large sheets of paper on it. Mix four different colors of washable paint and put each in a shallow tray. Tell the children to choose a color and then, in bare feet, to step into the tray of paint and to walk carefully along the paper, making footprints. When dry, display the footprints on the wall.
- Draw the foot shapes of some different animals and ask the children to guess which animal made the prints, such as round prints from an elephant, arrow prints from a bird, a pad and four toe prints from a dog, or flat, webbed triangular prints from a duck.